COMMUNITY · CONNECTIONS

HOW DO THEY HELP?
THE UNITED NATIONS

BY KATIE MARSICO

CHERRY
LAKE
Publishing

Published in the United States of America by Cherry Lake Publishing
Ann Arbor, Michigan
www.cherrylakepublishing.com

Content Adviser: Cynthia Rathinasamy, Master of Public Policy, Concentration in
International Development, Gerald R. Ford School of Public Policy,
The University of Michigan, Ann Arbor, MI
Reading Adviser: Marla Conn, ReadAbility, Inc.

Photo Credits: ©UN Photo/Sylvain Liechti, cover, 1, 17; ©UN Photo/Mark Garten, 5;
©Natalia Bratslavsky/Shutterstock Images, 7; ©Library of Congress/LC-USW33-054418-ZD, 9;
©Library of Congress/LC-USE6-D-009131, 11; ©UN Photo/Amanda Voisard,13;
©wweagle/iStock, 15; ©Sudan Envoy/http://www.flickr.com/CC-BY-2.0, 19;
©UN Photo/Shareef Sarhan, 21

LIBRARY OF CONGRESS CATALOGING-IN-PUBLICATION DATA
Marsico, Katie, 1980-
  The United Nations / by Katie Marsico.
     pages cm. — (Community connections)
  Includes bibliographical references and index.
  ISBN 978-1-63188-032-2 (hardcover) — ISBN 978-1-63188-075-9 (pbk.) —
ISBN 978-1-63188-118-3 (pdf) — ISBN 978-1-63188-161-9 (ebook)
  1. United Nations. 2. Disaster relief. 3. Peace. I. Title.
  JZ4984.5.M37 2015
  341.23—dc23   2014006221

Cherry Lake Publishing would like to acknowledge the
work of The Partnership for 21st Century Skills. Please
visit www.p21.org for more information.

Printed in the United States of America
Corporate Graphics Inc.

THE UNITED NATIONS

CONTENTS

HELP AND INTERNATIONAL HOPE

Life in a Syrian **refugee** camp is dangerous and uncertain. People there face daily threats such as hunger and illness. Yet a war in Syria has forced millions of refugees to flee their homeland.

Organizations such as the United Nations (UN) work hard to help refugees.

The UN provides refugees with food, medical care, and other help.

THINK!

Imagine life as a refugee. Illness and dirty living conditions are not unusual. Many refugee children sleep in tents or on cement floors. How do you think refugees feel about organizations such as the UN?

The UN is a group of 193 independent nations. This organization has four main purposes. The first is to spread world peace. The second is to build friendships between different countries. The third is to fight **poverty**, hunger, and disease while supporting education and **human rights**. The fourth is to help world nations join together to achieve these goals.

The flags of member nations fly in front of UN headquarters.

Try to guess which nations are members of the UN. See if you are able to name at least 10 besides Canada and the United States!

7

THE PAST AND PRESENT

World leaders formed the UN to deal with an international **crisis**. Between 1939 and 1945, World War II raged between two groups of countries. The first group was known as the Allied forces. The second was called the Axis powers. Allied leaders believed the Axis governments were a threat to global peace and **security**.

Allied forces included the United States, Canada, and Great Britain. Axis powers included Germany, Japan, and Italy.

LOOK!

Find photos of scenes from World War II. Try looking on the Internet or in books or magazines. Why do you think Allied leaders viewed this war as an international crisis?

In early 1942, representatives of 26 Allied nations gathered in Washington, D.C. President Franklin Delano Roosevelt unofficially referred to the countries represented at the meeting as the "United Nations."

By May 1945, World War II was over. Yet world leaders understood that they still needed to protect international peace and human rights. So, on October 24, 1945, they formally created the UN.

People still suffered from injuries after World War II ended.

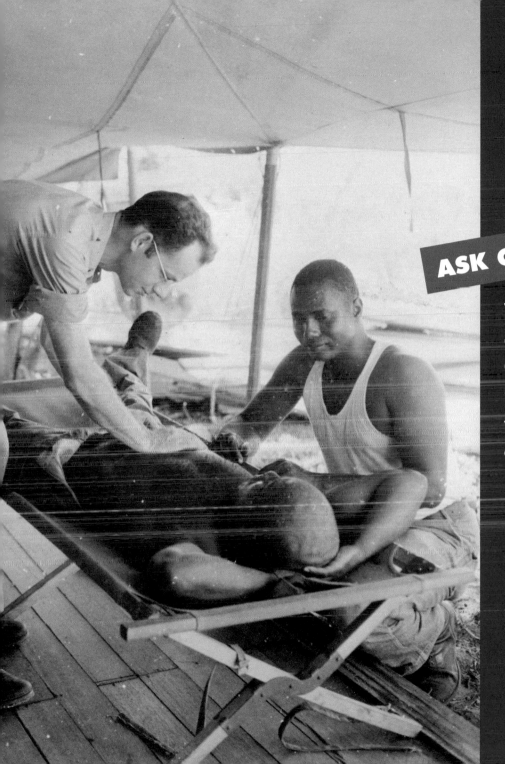

ASK QUESTIONS!

Want to know more about World War II? Can you find out who finally won? What was the turning point of the war?

11

At first, the UN was made up of only 51 countries. Since 1945, however, 142 other nations have joined. UN headquarters, or main offices, are located in New York City, New York.

The UN features six main branches, or parts. People are often most familiar with the General Assembly. All 193 nations participate in the Assembly. Officials in this branch discuss issues and make decisions that allow the UN to carry out its goals.

During UN meetings officials from the same continent sit together.

How can people from 193 different nations communicate during meetings? The UN's official languages are: Arabic, Chinese, English, French, Russian, and Spanish. As the speaker talks, his or her words are translated into those languages.

About 44,000 people work for the UN. Some are teachers, doctors, lawyers, and judges. These UN employees work at the main UN offices in New York, Switzerland, Austria, and Kenya, and in other locations.

Other workers are peacekeepers. UN peacekeepers include police officers, soldiers, and **civilians**. They make sure that life stays as orderly and calm as possible in troubled areas.

Peacekeepers often spend time in nations affected by wars or disaster.

LOOK!

Head to your local library or go online with a parent or teacher. See if you can find at least three places where UN peacekeepers are working. Now locate them on a map.

15

A WIDE RANGE OF WORK

The UN tries to find peaceful solutions to international problems. Officials organize inspections when they believe a country is building up weapons or preparing for an attack. UN peacekeepers often enter war-torn areas to urge military forces to **disarm**.

Peacekeepers often try to stop wars before they even start.

Are you able to guess how the UN pays for so many international projects? If you said that the money comes from its member nations, you're right! Both the United States and Canada are among the top 10 countries providing funding to the UN.

Member nations also work together to oppose terrorism. This is the use of violence or terror to achieve a political goal.

Other UN efforts involve human rights. Peacekeepers try to protect refugees from violence. Officials also encourage democracy. A democratic government gives citizens a voice and guarantees that they enjoy certain basic rights and freedoms.

The UN gives people hope for the future.

ASK QUESTIONS!

Do you want to work for the UN one day? Asking questions is the best way to learn about possible career paths. You could write, e-mail, phone, or visit UN headquarters in New York City.

Finally, the UN aids countries affected by natural disaster, disease, and poverty. UN workers help build— or sometimes rebuild—farms, businesses, schools, and hospitals.

The UN's efforts today mean a safer, more peaceful tomorrow for **generations** to come.

UN efforts help children today become the leaders of tomorrow.

Talk to teachers at your school about forming a model UN! A model UN encourages kids to learn about and discuss international issues affecting the world today.

21

GLOSSARY

civilians (suh-VILL-yuhnz) people who are neither soldiers nor police officers

crisis (KRY-suhss) a difficult or dangerous situation that usually requires immediate attention

disarm (dis-ARM) to set aside or reduce a supply of weapons

generations (jeh-nuh-RAY-shuhnz) groups of people who are born and live at about the same time

human rights (HYOO-muhn RYTES) rights that every person is entitled to as a human being

poverty (PAH-vuhr-tee) the state of being poor

refugee (reh-fyoo-JEE) someone who is forced to leave his or her homeland because of war or for political or religious reasons

security (sih-KYOOR-uh-tee) the state of being safe or protected from violence and destruction

FIND OUT MORE

BOOKS

Callery, Sean. *World War II*. New York: Scholastic, 2013.

Every Human Has Rights: A Photographic Declaration for Kids Based on the United Nations Universal Declaration of Human Rights. Washington, DC: National Geographic, 2009.

Harris, Joseph. *What Are Human Rights?* Mankato, MN: Arcturus Publishing, 2011.

WEB SITES

United Nations—CyberSchoolBus
cyberschoolbus.un.org
Visit this kid-friendly Web site for fast facts on both the UN and its current international programming.

Youth for Human Rights International—Learn Your Human Rights
www.youthforhumanrights.org/what-are-human-rights/universal-declaration-of-human-rights/articles-1-15.html
Check out this Web page for an easy-to-understand version of the UN's Universal Declaration of Human Rights. The declaration outlines the basic rights every person is entitled to.

INDEX

ABOUT THE AUTHOR

Katie Marsico is the author of more than 150 children's books. She lives in a suburb of Chicago, Illinois, with her husband and children.

24